M000308326

SPECTACULAR GOLF

PACIFIC NORTHWEST

THE MOST SCENIC AND CHALLENGING GOLF HOLES
IN WASHINGTON, OREGON, AND IDAHO

Published by

PANACHE

P A N A C H E   P A R T N E R S

Panache Partners Canada Inc.
469.246.6060
Fax: 469.246.6062
www.panache.com

Publishers: Brian G. Carabet and John A. Shand

Copyright © 2014 by Panache Partners, LLC
All rights reserved.

No part of this book may be reproduced or transmitted in any form or by any means,
electronic or mechanical, including photocopying, recording or by any information
storage or retrieval system, except brief excerpts for the purpose of review, without
written permission of the publisher.

All images in this book have been reproduced with the knowledge and prior consent
of the professionals and companies concerned and no responsibility is accepted by the
producer, publisher, or printer for any infringement of copyright or otherwise arising
from the contents of this publication. Every effort has been made to ensure that credits
accurately comply with the information supplied.

Printed in Malaysia

Distributed by Independent Publishers Group
800.888.4741

PUBLISHER'S DATA

Spectacular Golf Pacific Northwest

Library of Congress Control Number: 2014943280

ISBN 13: 978-0-9886140-6-2
ISBN 10: 0988614065

First Printing 2014

10 9 8 7 6 5 4 3 2 1

Right: Tetherow Golf Club, page 113

Previous Page: The Resort at the Mountain, page 109

This publication is intended to showcase golf courses and their signature holes. The
publisher does not require, warrant, endorse, or verify any professional accreditations,
educational backgrounds, or professional affiliations of the individuals or companies
included herein. All copy and photography published herein has been reviewed and
approved as free of any usage fees or rights and accurate by the individuals and/or
companies included herein.

Panache Partners, LLC, is dedicated to the restoration and conservation of the
environment. Our books are manufactured with strict adherence to an environmental
management system in accordance with ISO 14001 standards, including the use
of paper from mills certified to derive their products from well-managed forests.
We are committed to continued investigation of alternative paper products and
environmentally responsible manufacturing processes to ensure the preservation of our
fragile planet.

SPECTACULAR GOLF

PACIFIC NORTHWEST

FOREWORD

Growing up in Oregon gave me a healthy appreciation for every aspect of the game and helped me learn how to hit just about every shot in the bag: high shots; low shots; hooks; slices; bump and run shots; uphill, downhill, and side hill shots; and shots played in high winds and heavy rain. While most every region in the union brags about the "golf IQ" of their residents, I can confidently say that golfers in the Pacific Northwest have the know-how to compete on every course throughout the world.

My first experiences with golf were all family outings with my parents, brothers, and sister, where I had the chance to play classic courses like Columbia Edgewater Country Club, Eugene Country Club, Portland Golf Club, and Waverley Country Club. Golf was a game to be shared and enjoyed, and my parents made sure that even while in the competitive arena, we were taught first and foremost to respect the game: the rules, the etiquette, and, most importantly, the people who played it.

My first memories of professional golf in the area were of the Portland Opens and the Alcan Golfer of the Year Championship, both played at the legendary Portland Golf Club. From the 1947 Ryder Cup matches to the LPGA's Safeway Classic, the many USGA Championships, the uniquely fun Fred Meyer Challenge events, and the 2015 U.S. Open at Chambers Bay near Tacoma, professional golf in the Pacific Northwest has been as strong and varied as anywhere in the United States.

This landmark collection showcases the history, excitement, and diversity of golf experiences in the Pacific Northwest. Is there a more photographed hole than Coeur d'Alene Golf Resort's floating 14th? Or any more precise a course than Washington's Sahalee Country Club, with its iconic towering firs? From high plains desert courses in Oregon to mountain layouts in Washington and Idaho to the breathtakingly beautiful tracks on the Oregon coast, the golf experience is as different as you can get—all of it fun and rewarding.

Yours truly,

Peter Jacobsen

Peter Jacobsen

PGA

Pacific Northwest Section

On February 6, 1922, eight PGA professionals met in Seattle to form the Pacific Northwest Section of the PGA of America. Later in September, these same professionals organized the first Washington Open at the then nine-hole Yakima Country Club. Al Espinosa of Inglewood won the inaugural championship, besting the field at 282—for his effort, he took home the princely sum of $600. This early success led to the vibrant, professional association we see today.

Since those early years, the Pacific Northwest Section has fulfilled its mission to grow the game, teach the game, and play the game. Thanks to world-class programs developed in conjunction with the PGA of America, PGA professionals in the Pacific Northwest are recognized as the experts in the game and business of golf.

The Pacific Northwest Section encompasses Washington, Oregon, northern Idaho, western Montana, and Alaska, and represents 1,100 PGA professionals at the finest facilities in the region. The section conducts 225 events during the season, with the four major championships the most visible elements of the schedule. The Washington Open, Oregon Open, Northwest Open, and Rosauers Open feature the best players in the section and annually raise valuable resources for local charities. Total donations to these important organizations exceeded $650,000 in 2012 thanks to the efforts of the section and its sponsors.

The golf courses featured in this volume are some of the finest courses anywhere in the world and represent the quality, challenge, and variety of facilities found throughout the section. Whether it's the tall trees of western Washington, the seaside links on the Oregon Coast, or the high desert of central Oregon, we hope you enjoy these facilities not only through this publication but through a personal visit in the near future. Our PGA professionals will be there to welcome you and make your experience an enjoyable one.

Photographs courtesy of Pacific Northwest Section PGA

CONTENTS

The Cedars at Dungeness, page 21

Apple Tree Golf Course, page 71

WASHINGTON

Chambers Bay, page 75

AVALON GOLF LINKS
North Course

PAR 5 ◆ 595 YARDS

Burlington, WA
360.757.1900
www.avalonlinks.com

A family-owned facility, Avalon Golf Links was built by golfers, for golfers on a tranquil high-ground piece of property at the north end of the Skagit Valley. The Hass family saw a need for better public golf in the Puget Sound region and filled it in the early 1990s with 27 holes designed by Robert Muir Graves. Accomplished was a course challenging enough to host US Open qualifying tournaments but friendly enough to be enjoyed by all.

Avalon was designed to be demanding off the tee, and the sixth North fits that billing. With trees on both sides, joined by a bunker protecting the right side of the fairway and a cedar limiting options on the left, players are wise to recognize it as three-shot par 5 and try to find the fairway off the tee. With the green well-protected by a large pond, reaching the green in two requires a strong breeze at your back and two muscular shots. Few succeed, as the reward doesn't justify the risk.

The second shot is also demanding, since the fairway slopes from left to right with a pond awaiting any shots that bleed to the right. Hitting a longer second shot is advantageous, as the deeper you advance down the fairway the better the angle is on your third shot.

Photograph by Kamriell Welty

BEAR MOUNTAIN RANCH

Golf Course

18 HOLE

PAR 5 ◆ 690 YARDS

Chelan, WA
509.682.8200
www.bearmt.com

The 18th hole at Bear Mountain Ranch Golf Course will leave you with a memorable and lasting image of beauty and elegance. The par 5 measures 482 yards from the forward tees to a little over 690 yards from the back tees. Almost a quarter-mile of beautifully maintained turf finishes off the visually stunning day where the pristine, 55-mile long Lake Chelan and the Cascade Mountains are seen on every hole.

This memorable 18th ends with an approach shot through a 40-yard-wide gap in the trees and over a stream to a gently rolling green. It is a demanding but fair hole, but some may have to lay up on their third shot short of the stream and hope for an accurate fourth shot to attain par. Birdies are possible, but every shot must be hit accurately and not lack for distance.

Designed and built by Don Barth, the course is known beyond its vistas for its excellent GPS system, overall turf conditions, and multiple tees, stretching from 5,063 yards to a whopping 7,213 yards.

Bear Mountain Ranch adds to the growing collection of golf courses in the sunlit area of Lake Chelan, including Alta Lake, Desert Canyon, and Rock Island.

Photograph by Rob Perry

BROADMOOR
Golf Club

18 HOLE

PAR 5 ◆ 485 YARDS

Seattle, WA
206.325.5600
www.broadmoorgolfclub.com

Broadmoor Golf Club is a private club just minutes from downtown Seattle—so close, in fact, to Husky Stadium on the University of Washington campus that on specific Saturday afternoons the UW band sounds as if it is marching across the driving range. The 18th hole is a majestic finish for a majestic course; a par 5 where, despite the beauty and challenge that comes from a pond left of the hole and Lake Washington to the right, it is the grand clubhouse just up the hill from the green that you remember most.

Built in the 1920s by the esteemed designer A.V. Macan, Broadmoor has a rich history. It has been the site of the Seattle Open multiple times and is most noted for Byron Nelson's win there in 1945, when his 21-under-par total of 261 was a PGA record. In 1954, Bing Crosby and Jack Benny came to Broadmoor to play in the Western Amateur, and the 1962 Seattle Open celebrated the staging of the World's

Fair with a field that included pros Arnold Palmer, Bill Casper, Tony Lema, and Ken Venturi, and amateurs Bob Hope and James Garner. A young pro named Jack Nicklaus won the tournament.

More recently, England's Paul Casey shot 60 for 18 holes en route to winning the Pac-10 championship. He had a 25-foot putt for eagle on the 18th hole and a 59. For better players, the 485-yard 18th is a two-shot hole, but the risk of being short is a dip in the pond; for a shot that goes long, a chip down a slick green is almost impossible to hold. The long look to the iconic clubhouse is so captivating that few visitors know that they are walking three feet below the level of Lake Washington and on a seven-acre wetlands preserve—or really care.

Photographs by Rob Perry

CANYON LAKES
Golf Course

PAR 5 ◆ 527 YARDS

Kennewick, WA
509.582.3736
www.canyonlakesgolfcourse.com

The bold design at Canyon Lakes Golf Course means that sooner or later there comes a moment of truth, and it can come as early as the ninth hole, a devilish par 5 that commands respect and often your golf ball. Rated consistently among the best golf courses in Washington—4.5 stars by *Golf Digest* magazine—Canyon Lakes' 1981 design by local architect John Steidel rewards length and precision. With two-thirds of its play coming from an active membership, the majority of players know to respect the ninth hole, originally conceived as Canyon Lakes' finishing hole until the nines were flipped.

From an elevated tee, the drive must avoid a row of trees on the right and a steep bank falling down a hillside on the left. True drama lies ahead with an hourglass-shaped green behind a large, rock-faced pond that totals more than 50 yards long and annually attracts as many as 10,000 stray balls. The green is trapped left and enjoys the protection of the pond on the right, leaving players with either a heroic second shot or a well-played third to keep from adding to the watery casualty list. Steidel did provide a single land route to the green, but the winding path left of the hole is no easy target either. Once on the green, getting the ball in the hole is the challenge.

Canyon Lakes is most noted for its large, undulating greens, which at high speeds can be about as tough as they come. As they say, if you can putt at Canyon Lakes, you can putt anywhere.

Photograph courtesy of Canyon Lakes Golf Course

THE CEDARS AT DUNGENESS

3 HOLE

PAR 5 ◆ 490 YARDS

Sequim, WA
360.683.6344
www.cedarsatdungeness.com

What began as a simple farmland golf course 42 years ago has since morphed into a truly memorable golfing experience. Much of the allure surrounding The Cedars at Dungeness lies in its uniquely dry playing conditions—virtually unheard of near Seattle—which allow it to be billed as western Washington's driest course.

The signature hole on this gorgeous course is the third, appropriately named "Ole Crabby." It stretches to 490 yards from the tips, but don't let the length fool you—this is a formidable challenge. As you approach the tee, it is easy to be distracted by the majestic beauty of the Olympic Mountains. However, once you regain your composure, you'll want to aim the tee shot at the three fir trees at the end of the fairway. The fairway landing area appears to have ample room until you notice the enormous fairway bunker guarding the right side and out-of-bounds left. As you gaze west for your next shot, you encounter one of the world's truly memorable golfing hazards: a giant Dungeness crab-shaped bunker filled with red volcanic cinders from Bend, Oregon.

The big hitters have a chance to carry the ball 225 yards over the bunker. However, if trying to pick the right club to avoid the bunker's massive center or 10 legs wasn't daunting enough, you'll now have to negotiate the Juan de Fuca trade winds. The intelligent play for most is to lay up and try to hit a wedge over the bunker, but this too can prove intimidating, as the occasional high-pitched squeaking noises coming from a nearby Bald Eagle perch make the approach a little unnerving. Once safely on, take a deep breath and enjoy the gentle slope and true rolling green; with unfaltering confidence you can now boast to your friends that you conquered Ole Crabby.

Photograph by William Wright Photography

COLUMBIA POINT
Golf Club

PAR 5 ◆ 596 YARDS

Richland, WA
509.946.0710
www.playcolumbiapoint.com

When the city of Richland wanted to build an upscale public course, it hired Jim Engh, an architect whose work is now known worldwide, to design it. Columbia Point Golf Club was completed in 1997, and since then a generation of players has enjoyed its four water features, massive greens, sparkling white sand bunkers, beautifully sculpted fairways, and even its ninth hole.

Now here is a risk/reward hole, with the emphasis on "risk." The long par 5—596 yards from the tips—is played downwind, but even so the second shot is risky whether you mean for it to be or not. From an elevated tee box, the drive should be slightly to the right side of the fairway to open up the remainder of the hole. There are trees left and out-of-bounds. Even after a large tee shot, the second demands a 200-yard carry past water to the right-front of the green and out-of-bounds to the left.

A smarter play is aiming short of the water, but beware: The landing area slopes toward the water and anything hit with a hint of fade can be fatal. Columbia Point is part of a wonderful golf experience in the Tri-Cities area of southeast Washington, near the Columbia River and rolling hillsides of the growing wine industry. Within 50 miles there are 150 wineries—and almost that many golf holes.

Photograph courtesy of Columbia Point Golf Club

DESERT CANYON GOLF RESORT
Desert Nine

PAR 5 ◆ 690 YARDS

Orondo, WA
509.784.1234
www.desertcanyon.com

Hang on to your hat. Arguably the most photographed hole in eastern Washington, the celebrated par 5 at Desert Canyon Golf Resort is an epic journey covering more than 600 yards. Even without the expansive view of the mighty Columbia River below, the sixth hole on the Desert Nine would be unrivaled.

The drive is from an elevated tee teetering on the edge of the canyon to a restricted area that suggests—despite its length—that better players hit a three-wood. The temptation is to keep the drive right, but there is as much trouble right as there is left. Ahead is a quarter mile to be negotiated with big clubs and big dreams. The third shot to the green—usually a couple hundred yards long—must avoid a sheer drop off left and a bunker and collection area right.

It might as well be a par 6, but who is counting? The point is that Desert Canyon is a wild ride through a massive countryside of orchards and tumbleweeds—the dream course of the late Jack Frei, who designed and built it after successes on the west side of the mountains with Bear Creek, Echo Falls, and McCormick Woods. While it has a links look, the course is more target golf—more like the courses in Arizona—although Frei made fairways, as in links golf, as wide and forgiving as he could. Desert Canyon earned the number seven spot in *Golfweek* magazine's prestigious ranking of best in the state.

With good on-site lodging, and near other top courses—Alta Lake, Bear Mountain Ranch, and Gamble Sands—Desert Canyon can prove to be the perfect place for an extended golf gathering.

Photograph courtesy of Desert Canyon Golf Resort

EAGLEMONT
Golf Club

14 HOLE

PAR 5 ◆ 552 YARDS

Mount Vernon, WA
360.424.0800
www.eaglemontgolf.com

High in the hills above the town of Mount Vernon is Eaglemont Golf Club, known for its spectacular views and layout. John Steidel did the design in the early '90s, and it was a rigorous test of his abilities to negotiate elevation changes and intruding wetlands. The 14th hole, with a commanding view of Mount Baker to the north, does both with ample adventure, skirting two ravines and encouraging the best players to go for the green on the par 5 in two.

There are five sets of tees on the 14th—from 552 yards to 450 yards—to address different abilities, but in almost every case the first ravine must be crossed with the second shot. To take on the second ravine is sure risk and reward. Laying up near a stump to the left of the hole and avoiding the second ravine are prudent. Even if the ravines are avoided, the green is protected by a bunker on the left and has a severe slope from back to front. The key third shot, from near the stump, is still a good 150-yard poke.

Eaglemont, often rated among the 10 best public courses in Washington, is in its own world; every hole isolated and unique. Over its two decades, trees and bunkers have been removed to make the course more playable, but no less spectacular. Speaking of spectacular, a sprawling clubhouse was also added to properly begin and end each round of golf.

Photograph courtesy of Eaglemont Golf Club

GLENDALE
Country Club

PAR 5 ◆ 515 YARDS

Bellevue, WA
425.746.7944
www.glendalecc.com

When the Washington State Open is played at Glendale Country Club—and it often is—the final hole on the final day is, believe it or not, played shorter than longer. The seductive 18th hole on the tree-lined Bellevue course becomes tantalizingly reachable, as moving the tee forward makes it a 485-yard par 5 instead of its normal 515 yards from the tips. But to get to the green in two you must carry a pond that slips stealthily into the fairway and is only a few feet from a front-left pin placement. The "do-I-go-or-do-I-lay up?" decision has faced most of the state's good players and even one of its great ones. In 1978, Fred Couples, then a shaggy-haired 18-year-old amateur, won the Washington State Open at Glendale wearing, of all things, tennis shoes.

Couples shot 65 the final day to win the Open by a stroke. He overwhelmed the tight, tough course by hitting a 3-wood off the tee on most holes; a 3-wood in the pre-high-tech era that still traveled the best part of 280 yards. Glendale has become a popular tournament course, especially for the most important annual event in the state of Washington, holding the State Open 13 times.

The 18th hole becomes pivotal, with the leaders protecting their positions by being prudent, and the challengers going all out to get the ball on the green in two. In 2008, veteran pro Tim Berg saw his hopes of winning the Open go plop as he pulled his 185-yard second shot into the pond, losing a playoff to Brian Nosler. Meanwhile, Nosler's 4-iron from 208 yards landed softly on the green and he two-putted for birdie and the championship.

Glendale has surprising elevation changes and is noted for its small, speedy greens, making the course as delicate as it is delightful.

Photographs by Rob Perry

THE GOLF CLUB AT NEWCASTLE
Coal Creek Course

PAR 5 ◆ 621 YARDS

Newcastle, WA
425.793.5566
www.newcastlegolf.com

People flock to see the majestic clubhouse at The Golf Club at Newcastle and its incredible view beyond: a 200-degree panorama of Seattle, Bellevue, two floating bridges, freshwater lakes, a saltwater sea, and the serrated and frosted outline of the Olympic Mountains. While the scene mesmerizes everyone from diners to wedding reception attendees, the reality of Newcastle's Coal Creek course as a precise and formidable test of golf comes as soon as the opening hole.

The par 5 first demands probably more thinking and execution than those still infatuated with the view want to deal with, but there it is: a 621-yard hole that requires three brave but careful shots. Hit it farther than 250 yards from the tee and you bound into a wetlands area. Even landing just short of the wetlands and in prime position leaves you with a downhill lie for a lengthy second shot over a hazard to a gradually narrowing area 100 yards or more from the green. There is a creek on the left, mounds on the right, and even if you've eluded those, your third shot is to a green that is bisected front to back with a devilish mound.

The property at Newcastle opened in 1999 and features two 18-hole courses on a commanding 350-acre site. The Newcastle project was the fulfillment of former Microsoft executive Scott Oki's dream to bring high-end public golf to the Seattle area. Including Newcastle, Oki Golf now owns and operates eight other properties in Washington's Puget Sound region.

Photographs by Rob Perry

PALOUSE RIDGE
Golf Club

PAR 5 ◆ 626 YARDS

Pullman, WA
509.335.4342
www.palouseridge.com

The vastness of eastern Washington and northern Idaho, framed by the sensuous, rolling landscape of the Palouse, is the view at Palouse Ridge Golf Club on the campus of Washington State University. Somehow the carry to the fairway on the 10th hole is secondary to the view; the beauty more alluring than the beast in the 626-yard par 5. While the tee shot is more exhilarating than it is demanding, it is the second shot that separates the eagle-seekers from the tourists.

Architect John Harbottle III wanted the hole to blend into the horizon—a panorama that includes 4,500-foot Moscow Mountain in the neighboring state of Idaho. With an artist's eye, Harbottle matched curves and angles of the hole with the famous glacier-formed terrain. In fact, with the wind at your back, the tee shot can be hit too far, riding a slope to a point where you can't see the green. The second shot is hit over a small knob left of the green, and from there the ball can run toward the hole. Anything hit right of the green is trouble. The longest hitters will have a chance to reach the green in two despite its length, while mere mortals will be left with a nifty bump-and-run chip for a third shot.

The green, which surprisingly commands the same kind of view as does the tee, has its own challenges, including a back pin placement that seems to simply fall off the ridge. Palouse Ridge, which opened in 2008, replaced a funky nine-hole campus course and is now regarded as one of the top five university courses in the country.

Photographs by Rob Perry

SEATTLE GOLF CLUB

PAR 5 ◆ 511 YARDS

Seattle, WA
206.363.8811
www.seattlegolfclub.com

The ninth hole at Seattle Golf Club is an unforgettable glimpse into another time and another era. Out of the towering stands of fir and cedars you are suddenly confronted by the magnificent old clubhouse where members used to stay overnight because the trip back downtown was so far.

An uphill par 5, the ninth plays long but is reachable in two shots for a long hitter. The problem is a narrow opening to a green, guarded by bunkers left and right, and a putting surface that can demand an approach shot be on the same level as the pin placement, or be the start of a three-putt birdie-turned-bogey result.

But no matter the result, the lasting memory is of the clubhouse. So much at Seattle Golf Club is about history and tradition, and nothing captures it better than the chalet-style clubhouse. Its predecessors were a tent for the original, turn-of-the-century clubhouse near Gas Works Park in downtown Seattle, and then a family residence for the expansion to the Lake Washington neighborhood of Laurelhurst. Built in 1908 on a site north of the city by Cutter & Malmgren—the architects of The Rainier Club and the Stimson-Green Mansion on First Hill—today's clubhouse retains its original purpose as a vacation-style lodge. It features spacious banquet facilities and decks with magnificent views: west to Puget Sound and the Olympic Mountains, east to the course. The clubhouse underwent a massive overhaul in the 1980s but never forgot the style and simplicity that its founders wanted.

Over the years, Seattle Golf Club has worked at perpetuating amateur golf in the Northwest as host of the 1952 US Amateur, the 1961 Walker Cup, the 1981 US Senior Championship, and the 2010 Men's Pac-10 Conference Championship.

Photograph by Bryce Schoonmaker

TACOMA
Country & Golf Club

16 HOLE

PAR 5 ◆ 500 YARDS

Lakewood, WA
253.588.2161
www.golftcgc.com

Some of architect John Harbottle III's best, and sadly final design, work can be seen on the 16th hole at Tacoma Country & Golf Club, a venerable place where four-time Major champion James Barnes was the pro from 1910 to 1915. The workers of Scottish companies in Puget Sound first played golf on prairie lands south of Tacoma in 1892, and two years later formed Tacoma Golf Club, making it the first golf club in the western United States. In 1904, the golf club merged with Tacoma Country Club on the shores of American Lake. Updates by the likes of Harbottle, along with wonderful turf conditions and practice facilities, have lured touring pros such as Andres Gonzales, Troy Kelly, Ryan Moore, Michael Putnam, and Kyle Stanley into becoming members.

The 16th hole is a reachable par 5 if you've driven the ball in the fairway. The second shot suggests a fade into a green tucked

into a hollow, but large trees on the left side of the fairway prevent that. What remains is a shot working left over two bunkers redesigned by Harbottle, who grew up on the course, and whose parents—themselves national championship players—still live on the course.

Tacoma Country & Golf Club is one of the great places to play golf in the Northwest; a peaceful, poetic place that is demanding without being demonic. The 16th hole is respectful of the grace and seductiveness of the remaining 17 holes.

Photograph by Dean Minor

WENATCHEE
Golf & Country Club

PAR 5 ◆ 486 YARDS

East Wenatchee, WA
509.884.7105
www.wenatcheegolfclub.org

A quick look at the scorecard does little justice to the challenge of Wenatchee Golf & Country Club. How difficult can a 6,400-yard golf course be? Difficult enough to host qualifying for the U.S. Amateur, that's how. In the pines not far from the Columbia River, Wenatchee is sneaky long, as they say, and it is just plain sneaky with its celebrated "small, firm, fast greens."

Originally designed in 1923 by the renowned architect A.V. Macan, Wenatchee has grown from nine to 18 holes with significant upgrades in the '90s by John Steidel. Its own version of Amen Corner comes with the 13th, 14th, and 15th holes, the 14th being a par 3 over water and the 15th a drivable par 4. But it all begins with the 13th, a 486-yard par 5 that requires precision whether you try to reach it in two shots or three. The false front—which makes it feel at times as though you are playing a Donald Ross design—rejects anything short of the green, chasing the ball back toward a swale. Ideally, those laying up need to be at the bottom of the swale to have the best chance to get a third shot close to the pin. Beware of the bunker on the left-front of the green and the trees behind it.

The putting surfaces are notoriously quick—almost slippery—and generally break toward the river, but not always. Wenatchee's big pines are not as pervasive as the firs across the mountains, but they are positioned to do more damage than can be imagined. This is a golf course that requires the precision of a jet pilot and the touch of a safecracker.

Photograph courtesy of Wenatchee Golf & Country Club

ALTA LAKE
Golf Course

PAR 4 ◆ 387 YARDS

Pateros, WA
509.923.2359
www.altalakegolf.com

As a golf writer once wrote about Alta Lake Golf Course, "I hate to give this one away." A course with a cult following, Alta Lake has stunning views of both the Columbia River and Alta Lake, and its mountain nine and desert nine are nothing short of scenic perfection. Adjacent to the town of Pateros, the north central Washington course was built in 1974 and then expanded to 18 holes in 1992 under the direction of Don Barth, who would later design his course at nearby Bear Mountain.

Generations of golfers have enjoyed Alta Lake, with one particular group of 40 playing every spring and fall since 1979. The finishing hole, the 387-yard 18th, offers expansive views of the Columbia from a green perched high on a rocky ridge. The hole doglegs left at a 90-degree angle, the last 150 yards uphill to a green that repels everything short, but also scares you to death with a putt from anything long. If you can't reach the dogleg with your drive, then a play over the sagebrush is long, but possible. Don't be right with the tee shot, because you'll end up out of bounds in an orchard.

Besides quick, runaway greens, the test at Alta Lake is getting a reservation at its adjoining 32-room motel. Nearly everyone who plays here stays here, and nearly everyone comes back for more. Fun, family, and a see-you-again-next-year mentality is the ethos of this place.

Photograph courtesy of Alta Lake Golf Course

CANTERWOOD
Golf & Country Club

PAR 4 ◆ 427 YARDS

Gig Harbor, WA
253.851.1845
www.canterwoodgcc.com

When the original owner, an Oregon lumberman, wanted to build one of the toughest golf courses in the country, renowned architect Robert Muir Graves did so—and then some. Now in its 25th season, Canterwood Golf & Country Club has undergone more than a few changes, most to make the course more playable for the average member. But the spirit of Graves' work remains in the form of huge tree stumps that tell of another time.

The 10th hole begs you to pick a route, either left or right of a stump in the middle of the fairway—smack in the middle. It doesn't matter so much which route you choose, although the better players will go left of the stump when the pin placement is on the right, and vice versa. But no matter what, avoid the stump. The 10th hole is a strong par 4, and the drive is crucial, as is picking the right tees from which to play the course. The tee shot is over two small lakes and into a hillside, unless, of course, you can carry it far enough to get a look at the green. Without an appropriate drive,

the second shot will be blind and more than 200 yards. And daunting. At one point, in the initial design, there was another tree 50 yards or so beyond the stump. Graves was asked to look at possible course modifications and, during a round of golf with club officials, found his ball lodged right behind the second tree. Within a few days, the tree ended up in someone's fireplace.

A major bunker/tee renovation project was completed in 2007 under the direction of John Harbottle III. With no need to add length to a course that measured more than 7,300 yards; the course was "shortened" dramatically with a new set of forward tees. At the same time, trees were removed to promote the growing of better turf, and brush on the perimeters was removed. The tree at the 10th? It perseveres.

Photograph courtesy of Canterwood Golf & Country Club

THE LINKS
at Moses Pointe

PAR 4 ◆ 423 YARDS

Moses Lake, WA
866.764.2275
www.mosespointe.com

The Links at Moses Pointe has its share of water, native grasses, and desert challenges, but only one hole that requires a forced carry over water to reach the green in regulation: the stunning 423-yard ninth hole. The blind tee shot is aided by a 150-yard pole and bunker on the right side of the fairway. A well-struck tee shot left of the 150 marker will leave one of the most memorable approach shots on any golf course in the Pacific Northwest.

Closely guarded by a small lake in front of the green and surrounded by tan-colored sand that highlights the native grasses framing the bunkers, this large and undulating green is the only refuge for the golfer's approach. The well-defined ridge that bisects this enormous green suggests to the better player the importance of staying below the hole. For most players, however, anywhere on the putting surface is a welcome thought compared to the alternatives.

More intimidating than difficult, the downhill approach shot to the ninth is typically a medium to short iron that plays about a club shorter. With Moses Lake as the backdrop and desert beauty all around, this breathtaking approach is just the challenge that golfers dream of conquering.

Photograph by JR Johnson, golfphotos.com

MERIDIAN VALLEY
Country Club

PAR 4 ◆ 426 YARDS

Kent, WA
253.631.3131
www.meridianvalleycc.com

Meridian Valley Country Club, for years one of the most popular stops on the LPGA Tour, remains an oasis in the East Hill area of Kent. But among the beauty is a beast: the 426-yard fifth hole, a par 4 that ranks as the toughest hole on the course for all the right reasons. It was first sketched by the esteemed architect Ted Robinson, who deemed the long, narrow par 4 difficult enough with a deep swale fronting a green cut into a hillside. A flood in the late 1990s washed out a culvert underneath the fairway, turning a swale into a stream. The members liked the look enough to fortify the creek banks of the newly minted hazard.

Without a nearly perfect tee shot, there is no chance to go for the green on the second shot. A huge tree blocks the left side of the fairway, and a bunker guards the right. The perfect tee shot is right to left away from the bunker, leaving 160 yards to a green that slopes precipitously to the creek. Most players opt to lay up, but still must be careful because anything within 75 yards of the creek leaves a downhill lie. The third shot—best played from 100 yards—won't be the easiest either, as anything long leaves a downhill putt as scary as it is subtle. Anything short is wet.

The winners during the 18-year run of the Safeco Classic were classic ball strikers, such as JoAnne Carner, Juli Inkster, Annika Sorenstam, Karrie Webb, and Kathy Whitworth. With a new $6 million clubhouse, Meridian Valley is better than ever and the fifth hole tougher than ever, all of which could help lure the LPGA Tour—which left only because sponsorship for its tournament did—back to the state of Washington.

Photograph by Mike Rucker

MOUNT SI
Golf Course

PAR 4 ◆ 350 YARDS

Snoqualmie, WA
425.391.4926
www.mtsigolf.com

When does a slight dogleg reveal a slight miracle? After rounding the bend at the sixth hole at Mount Si Golf Course. It's the start of a neck-craning look from the Snoqualmie Valley floor to the tip of Mount Si, a little over 4,000 feet straight up. About 10,000 hikers per year attempt the climb to the top—fewer than half actually make it. And if the mountain doesn't captivate, then the neighboring herd of elk just might.

For this is an amazing place; a pleasant public golf course at the base of the snowy Cascade Range and yet only a 30-minute drive from the steel-and-glass landscape of downtown Seattle. Standing on the tee, tall trees and surges of the south fork of the Snoqualmie River are to the right. The obvious play is to the left, and long hitters can drive the ball through the fairway. The hole dares you to get as close to the green as possible with the drive, as it narrows with poplar trees on the left and a big evergreen on the right. The more prudent play might be to hit a 5-wood or 3-wood short of the trouble and play a short iron to the green.

There are no bunkers near the green, just a swale in front to contain shots that fall short. The sixth isn't meant to be the toughest hole on the course—just the most beautiful.

Photograph by Meagan Barter

OVERLAKE
Golf and Country Club

18 HOLE

PAR 4 ◆ 424 YARDS

Medina, WA
425.454.7971
www.overlake.club

Although it is academically argued to this day which Overlake Golf and Country Club layout is the most representative of the surrounding Medina neighborhood, there is no argument about the influence of course designer A.V. Macan, one of the Northwest's most prolific and profound architects. Macan, an Irish immigrant who designed great Northwest courses ranging from Broadmoor, Fircrest, and Inglewood in Seattle to Marine Drive, Shaughnessy, and Victoria Royal Colwood in British Columbia, also designed the "new course" at Overlake in 1953 from scratch since the original 1927 Francis L. James layout did not survive the Depression.

The 18th hole at Overlake is a long par-4 crescendo that features another challenging site. A drive down the right side of the fairway opens up the best angle to the green because of the grove of Douglas fir trees guarding its short-left flank. Macan believed in holes that played as "hard 4s and easy 5s." This refers to the fact that many of his holes were extremely challenging to make pars, but through intelligent play were

relatively ·easy to make bogey. This green has long been controversial, especially as green speeds have become faster over time. Macan was a proponent of putting surfaces that challenge the best players but are receptive to a running approach shot, and nearly every green at Overlake exhibits this philosophy.

Renovating the 18th green has been a perennial discussion over the years to soften the slopes and make it a fairer finish. However, it was decided that rather than compromise the character of such an interesting green, the rough around the green would be cut down to fairway-height runoff areas to allow a broader variety of creative greenside approach shots. Juxtaposed with the usually boisterous gallery balcony of the clubhouse and pressed with such a strategic green, golfers leave the 18th green knowing they have been challenged by the best.

Photograph courtesy of Overlake Golf and Country Club

PLEASE USE
PERISCOPE
BEFORE TEEING

THE RESORT AT PORT LUDLOW
Tide Course

2 HOLE

PAR 4 ◆ 342 YARDS

Port Ludlow, WA
360.437.0272
www.portludlowresort.com

The Resort at Port Ludlow is home to a boutique waterfront inn, a 300-slip marina, and "the most scenic golf course in the world," according to *Esquire* magazine. Few who have been there would debate its beauty—not now nor in the '70s, when Port Ludlow opened as one of Washington's first resort golf courses. The celebrated Robert Muir Graves layout is sumptuous, boasting views of Hood Canal and Mount Baker, along with wonderful positioning of large, old-growth stumps, exotic blotches of wild flowers, and great golf holes. Port Ludlow is one of only 200 courses in the country to be certified with Audubon International and receive sanctuary status.

The course is comprised of 18 holes, known as Tide and Timber. One flows down toward the water and the other treks through a dense forest. The second hole on Tide pulls the whole picture into focus with a scenic overlook of the marina and inn below, as well as an early, unforgettable risk/reward hole. A big hitter can challenge this hole by aiming down the left-hand side guarded by an old-growth fir that acts like a catcher's mitt, poised to snatch an errant shot. Right is no bargain either, as any tee shot that direction might slip out of bounds or end up in a hazard. Most players choose to play this hole with a long iron or fairway metal to the large part of the fairway. Do this, and a short iron to an accessible green awaits. Just about every pin placement on this kidney-shaped green shouts "take dead aim," and birdies are possible.

Before playing this hole, always be sure to check that the fairway below is clear using the distinctive periscope located just to the left of the tee box.

Photographs courtesy of The Resort at Port Ludlow

ROCK ISLAND
Golf Course

PAR 4 ◆ 340 YARDS

Rock Island, WA
509.884.2806
www.rockislandgolfcourse.com

The past for Rock Island Golf Course includes the dramatic flooding of the original course when a dam backed up the Columbia River. The present might not be quite as dramatic, but you can't be sure of that walking onto the 11th tee when you see a lake sculpting the entire left side of the fairway.

The hole isn't long—340 yards for the big boys and 300 for the rest of us—but the temptation is always there to try to drive the green. A good, strong draw with the driver will get the job done, or so they say. A smarter play is to lay up to a good wedge distance while using a hillside along the right side of the fairway to get the ball in front of the green.

The evolution of Rock Island involves not only the drowning of the first course, but a rescue by the Barth family that included the recent addition of a second nine and a general revamping of all 18 holes. Don Barth, who also owns Alta Lake, Bear Mountain Ranch, and Desert Canyon, did the design and construction of the new holes with the help of superintendent and nephew Jon Roberts.

Amid huge ponds, Rock Island presents a formidable challenge. Its slope rating from the back tees is a healthy 129. Once you get past the 11th hole, along comes Don Barth's favorite, the 13th, a par 4 that makes a direct dogleg to the right and against where there is yet another pond: a true oasis or a watery grave.

Photograph courtesy of Rock Island Golf Course

ROYAL OAKS
Country Club

PAR 4 ◆ 392 YARDS

Vancouver, WA
360.256.1250
www.royaloaks.net

The current back nine at Royal Oaks Country Club was the first to be built in 1945; the front nine followed seven years later. Burnt Bridge Creek, which borders the third hole along the left edge of the fairway before crossing it 100 yards out from the green, was rerouted to accommodate the layout of this par 4 hole. The club's founders originally pledged 50 hours or $50 to remove the rocks, by hand, from the holes near the creek. Even with this effort, many members still kept two sets of clubs.

Native ash, oak, and fir trees frame the hole, intensifying the distinctive Pacific Northwest aura. The fairway doglegs slightly to the left and slopes from right to left off the tee to approximately 175 yards from the green, where it levels off. Targeting the stone bridge that crosses the creek on the right side of the hole is smart. A slight draw off the tee is the ideal shot to play the dogleg, using the natural slope of the hole and avoiding the creek on the left. Trees will block any second shot to the green for those who go long-right off the tee.

The green slopes steeply from back to front-right. Experienced players will sometimes even intentionally hit their approach shot short of the green rather than risk being above the hole. There are three green-side bunkers: a larger bunker on the left and two smaller ones on the right. Hitting out of the left bunker, it is especially difficult to stop the ball near the pin or just keep it on the green. Two large oak trees short-right of the green also make any shot in this area very challenging. Keep it below the hole, and you'll enjoy the outcome.

Photograph by Jeff Miller

SALISH CLIFFS
Golf Club

14 HOLE

PAR 4 ◆ 437 YARDS

Shelton, WA
360.462.3673
www.salish-cliffs.com

Owned and operated by the Squaxin Island Tribe, Salish Cliffs Golf Club is a stunning mountain layout with 600 feet of elevation change. It offers 360-degree views of the Kamilche Valley, immaculate conditioning, and the go-for-it-or-don't excitement of the 14th hole. The hole stretches to 437 yards—383 yards from the regular tees—and is often played into the wind, ending the temptation for most to try to reach the green in two shots. The peninsula green is surrounded by a wetlands area that offers no hope of escape.

Off the tee, Gene Bates has designed a shot that is reminiscent of a Herbert Strong hole, allowing you to see the fairway and observe much of the ball's flight until it disappears over a small crest. When you arrive at your tee shot, the grandeur of the hole is revealed as well as the decisions that must be made to deal with it. Balls in the fairway present the player with a mid- to long-iron or hybrid approach to the green. It is all carry from 175 to 200 yards. Those missing the fairway or deciding not to attempt to reach the green can choose to lay up short of the green, but even the layup must be thought through and should take into account the hole location. If the pin is right, stay left, and vice versa.

Trying to knock the ball on the green in regulation gives a great thrill and a chance at a birdie. But many of the bold efforts lead to a quick double bogey, and in match play this hole is often won with a bogey made through safe, conservative play.

Photograph by Brian Oar

SUDDEN VALLEY
Golf Course

PAR 4 ◆ 421 YARDS

Bellingham, WA
360.734.6435
www.suddenvalleygolfcourse.com

Many changes have taken place at Sudden Valley Golf Course, but little has been done to the rapture that is the fifth hole. From the tee, a giant cherry tree on the left side of the fairway blocks not only errant tee shots, but views of the 12-mile-long Lake Whatcom. Get around the tree—it takes a 270-yard poke from the back tees—and the lake and the Cascade foothills behind it come stunningly into view.

Aesthetics aside, the 421-yard par 4 is Sudden Valley's number-one handicap hole. While it is temping to draw the ball around the tree and toward the hole with a driver, a more prudent play is hitting a 3-metal slightly right of the big tree to keep the tee shot from skipping into the tall fescue along the right edge of the fairway. The wind off the lake, always blowing harder at the hole than it is from where your tee shot landed, can wreak havoc with the second shot, and the green is among the largest on the course.

Sudden Valley was an early creation of Ted Robinson, and like all his designs, trees didn't simply frame holes but often defined them. The course was celebrated enough early on that it held the 1981 Washington State Open and Amateur, events won respectively by revered players Rick Acton and John Bodenhamer. No one ever talks about Sudden Valley without mentioning the differences between the two nines: one sweeping out to the lake, the other trail-blazing its way up and down a mountainside. Both, while different, are truly spectacular.

Photograph by Jim Smithson

SUNCADIA
Prospector Course

PAR 4 ◆ 410 YARDS

Cle Elum, WA
866.715.5050
www.suncadia.com

Seldom are golf holes breathtaking, as in standing on the rim of the Grand Canyon or viewing Crater Lake for the first time. Welcome to the 10th tee at Suncadia's Prospector Course. At first, you don't think too much about decoding the hole, figuring out if you can indeed fly the bunkers on the left to take a shorter path to the green. No, you want to record the moment before and after you hit the tee shot, taking in the colossal Cascade Mountains valley in front of you. In the distance are Mount Baldy, Domerie Peak, and glimpses of the Tumble Creek course across the Cle Elum River.

Back to the hole, the fairway is 130 feet below the tee. The vantage point suggests to swing away and not worry where it goes, but the reality is that a decision must be made. Can you clear the cluster of bunkers left to give you a shorter shot into the green? Or do you play carefully toward the right and wide-open right side of the fairway? Usually, the prevailing wind makes the decision. In your face, play safe. At

your back, go for it. Taking the shortcut is usually worth the risk, giving a much better entrance to the hole. Shots hit right and safe require a second shot that has to flirt with bunkers right of the green. The hole is nothing but fun, although getting to the green doesn't suggest that the struggle is over. Putting on the Arnold Palmer-designed Prospector Course is never without challenge.

Although Suncadia is only 80 miles from Seattle, it is a world away, with more sun and elevation, and less rain and turmoil. Recreation opportunities abound year-round and range from river rafting to snowshoeing. Included is another public-access golf course, Rope Rider. This is a spectacular setting for a spectacular resort.

Photographs courtesy of Suncadia

WHITE HORSE
Golf Club

PAR 4 ◆ 435 YARDS

Kingston, WA
360.297.4468
www.whitehorsegolf.com

White Horse Golf Club, a veritable collection of signature golf holes in the sandy hills above the coastal hamlet of Kingston, still saves the best for last. The 18th hole, arguably the best finishing hole in the Northwest, is a par 4 to remember, breaking free of the surrounding forests to embrace the picturesque two-and-a-half-acre lake bordering the entire left side of the fairway and framed by the club's majestic 20,000-square-foot clubhouse.

With the lake on the left, and bunkers and a grove of trees framing the right side of the fairway, the tee shot is not for the meek. And in order to have a user-friendly approach shot that doesn't require removing a headcover to go for the pin, the drive can't be about playing safe. That being said, White Horse Golf Club, the original design of Cynthia Dye McGarey, is truly a second-shot course with greens that are often oblique to the player's eye—greens difficult enough to make her famous uncle, Pete

Dye, envious. With water sculpting the green to the left and little layup area right, the shot to the 18th must be taken straight on, with the locals watching from the nearby deck of the new clubhouse. It's all pretty spectacular.

White Horse opened as *Golf Digest*'s number eight top new golf course in 2007. It underwent numerous challenges until finally being gathered up by the adjoining Suquamish Tribe. John Harbottle III did an extensive remodel of the course in 2011, removing nearly 60 bunkers and considerably more trees. It has since been honored as one of the state's top 10 courses you can play and is definitely worth adding to everyone's "must-play bucket list."

Photograph by Rob Perry

YAKIMA COUNTRY CLUB

PAR 4 ◆ 363 YARDS

Yakima, WA
509.452.2266
www.yakimacountryclub.org

Yakima Country Club is a desert oasis with more water than you can imagine for a valley east of the Cascade Mountains that averages seven inches of rainfall a year. When playing the eighth hole, there might be more water than you want and need. Designed originally in the 1920s by the great A.V. Macan, Yakima is a step back in time with its tree-lined fairways, small greens, stunning views of Mount Adams and Mount Rainier, and gracious clubhouse. Not surprisingly, Yakima rewards precise golf shots and, in some cases, demands them.

The eighth hole is a mid-range par 4 and a classic risk/reward. Water looms in front of the tee shot as golfers decide how to play the subtle dogleg. Those who choose to carry the drive over the water must contend with a very small landing area, not to mention the water. Players who are wise and lay up between 100 and 150 yards have the task of hitting a long iron between the water and a fairway sand trap, an area that is perhaps 15 yards wide. Another option is to lay back around 175 yards where there is no trouble, but that means hitting a longer shot to the green.

It takes golfers a lifetime to learn how to read Yakima Country Club's greens on their own, and this terraced green at the eighth has slopes in every direction—left to right, right to left, uphill and downhill—illustrating why two-putting is difficult on Yakima's unnerving undulations.

Photograph by Ronald Warninger

ALDARRA
Golf Club

PAR 3 ◆ 234 YARDS

Sammamish, WA
425.222.7828
www.aldarragolfclub.com

Aldarra Golf Club remains true to its mission to provide pure golf. No starting times, no swimming pool, no greens committee, few tournaments—just golf. And despite its inviting nature and grace, the course has teeth and a snarl, best represented by the 15th hole that triggers the home stretch or what the members call the "Gauntlet." There can be no more challenging par 3 in the Northwest than the 15th at Aldarra.

The purity of the hole begins on the tee. A tall tree on each side eliminates playing any kind of big slice or hook to the hole, which rests uneasily 234 yards from the back tee and 197 yards from the member tees. The next visual obstacle is a large, deep bunker protecting the middle of the green. Those who can't fly the bunker are pretty much out of luck, and those who can must still stop a 200-yard shot on a narrow, nasty green. Anything left and short of the bunker can roll 30 yards back toward the tee because of a false front; anything that misses the green right or long can find a hazard. The nostalgia offered by the grain silo to the left of the hole sometimes gets short shrift, as survival—not sentiment—is the primary instinct needed when playing the 15th.

Aldarra is a special course on a unique piece of property, one of the fine works by world-renowned architect Tom Fazio. It is at times a sprawling vestige of a Northwest farm, and at other times a tree-lined forest that dips in and out of valleys, the browns and reds of its fescue grasses set against a backdrop of snow-capped mountains— where the Gauntlet awaits.

Photograph by Rob Perry

APPLE TREE

Golf Course

PAR 3 ◆ 180 YARDS

Yakima, WA
509.966.5877
www.appletreeresort.com

Unlike the 17th at Sawgrass or the 13th at Coeur d'Alene, where during a round there is as much dread as there is anticipation, most look forward to the celebrated 17th hole at Apple Tree Golf Course. Only a few holes in golf are more recognizable than the Apple. It is picturesque, slightly outrageous, and very enjoyable to play. And it has attracted appropriate interest to the tumbling resort that winds its way through mature apple orchards west of Yakima, where long ago a desert was transformed into one of the world's prime fruit baskets. Irrigation—the channeled snow runoff waters of the nearby Cascade Mountains—turns the land lush and also provides for creeks and ponds.

The 17th at Apple Tree demands a group picture on the tee, just as it demands a clean, unwavering shot, whether you tee it up from the back tees at 180 yards or from the 110-yard front tees. The elevated tees show off the island green, but don't be tricked into choosing too little club to reach the quarter-of-an-acre green.

Visually the hole works because the leaf of the Apple is raised above the surface of the green and filled with white sand. The reality is, the green is easy to hit as long as you aren't distracted by the publicity surrounding the hole, and you aren't drawn to perimeter pin placements. Hit the ball in the middle of the green and enjoy one of golf's most enjoyable holes.

While the signature 17th at Apple Tree receives most of the attention, the rest of the championship track plays over 6,900 yards and features a variety of scenic challenges including lakes, fountains, and a beautiful cascading waterfall. Plus, with five different tee blocks, Apple Tree allows golfers of every level the opportunity to use every club in their bag.

Photograph courtesy of Apple Tree Golf Course

BEAR MOUNTAIN RANCH
Golf Course

PAR 3 ◆ 237 YARDS

Chelan, WA
509.682.8200
www.bearmt.com

Talk about an infinity hole; this is infinity and beyond. At the seventh hole at Bear Mountain Ranch, your first thought is not about club selection but rather how the green blends into the blue of Lake Chelan and Lake Chelan into the massive Cascade Mountains beyond.

Bear Mountain Ranch is the dream and design of Don Barth, who made golf holes where others made photographs. The seventh is a par 3 that can be played from as few as 100 yards to a back tee location of 237 yards. The hole plays downhill and over a small pond that suddenly, once you've surveyed the landscape, appears bigger than it is. There is no question you need a club to reach the green, but there lingers the fear of going too long. Right of the green is a bunker, and beyond is, well, beyond.

Orchards and vineyards help frame the hole on one of the most scenic spots of a very scenic—and challenging—course. Bear Mountain is noted for its wonderful, lush fairways and its prepared greens. Built in 2005, it was quickly recognized as one of the country's best new courses. There is no signature hole at Bear Mountain Ranch, but many of them. It is a signature golf course, able to accommodate even the very best players from a distance of 7,213 yards. It has an elevation loss of 700 feet from top to bottom, all of which at times seems to happen on the hole you're playing.

Photograph by Dean Crane

CHAMBERS BAY

PAR 3 ◆ 172 YARDS

University Place, WA
253.460.4653
www.chambersbaygolf.com

Eight months after it opened in 2007, Chambers Bay was awarded the 2015 U.S. Open. Not only the first course in the Northwest to host a U.S. Open, it's also only the third municipal course and the first built in almost 50 years to snag one—an unprecedented feat. The course proved worthy during the 2010 U.S. Amateur, and has since offered casual golfers the chance to play the same holes as Tiger Woods and Rory McIlroy.

The 15th is the most recognizable golf hole in the state of Washington, with stunning views of Puget Sound, McNeil Island, and the Olympic Mountains in the distance. To make it even more unforgettable, it's home to the Lone Fir, a symbol as iconic to Chambers Bay as the lighthouse is to Scotland's Turnberry Resort. While Chambers Bay is just beginning to establish the championship pedigree of other US Open sites, it has its own history as a 100-year-old sand and gravel mine. Even the tree has a story, having been vandalized in 2008 by an unknown intruder.

The hole sits like a postage stamp above the railroad tracks—but don't assume that the shortest par 3 on the course is also the easiest. With most play coming from about 120 yards, the hole demands a crisp shot into the wind, favoring the left half of the green even when the pin is to the right. There is a slope left of the green that can feed balls to the hole, a trick which led to a dozen holes-in-one during the course's first five years, two of which came on successive swings in the same group. If the pin is on the right, beware: a tongue of green laps down toward the giant waste area. Snap a picture, grab your wedge, note which way the wind is blowing, wonder what Tiger Woods would do, and enjoy one of golf's great new holes.

Photograph by Martin Miller

HIGHLANDER
Golf Course

9 HOLE

PAR 3 ◆ 179 YARDS

East Wenatchee, WA
509.884.4653
www.highlandergc.com

It feels as if you are standing on the rim of the world, some 800 feet above the massive Columbia River, all of which can make golf rather insignificant—for a moment, anyway. But the reality sinks in as you back away from the panorama and have to deal with the shot. There may be more notable par 3s in the Pacific Northwest, but there is none more commanding than the ninth at Highlander Golf Course, high in the orchards above East Wenatchee.

From the back tee, it is a 179-yard shot over a ravine. If you don't look down, the shot isn't terribly difficult on many days. But good players have hit everything from a pitching wedge to a 3-wood, depending on the sneaky winds that sweep through the Columbia River Valley, sometimes even undetected by the green's flag. A person with sense keeps his shot on the right half of the green, for the world seems to tilt left on this hole, the slope of the green heading a pulled tee shot toward a bunker if you're lucky, or to the Columbia River if you aren't. Play too safe right and you're saddled with a chip over a hump to a location that might be in a different ZIP code.

Highlander is an evolving golf course; the front nine has added trees and water features while losing gnarly pot bunkers and inescapable fescue grasses bordering the fairways. The back nine is due some of the same transformations, plus some hole relocations that will come with the building of homes along the edge of the course. All on the rim of the world.

Photograph by John R. Johnson, golfphotos.com

OVERLAKE
Golf and Country Club

PAR 3 ◆ 144 YARDS

Medina, WA
425.454.7971
www.overlake.club

The third hole at Overlake Golf and Country is the showpiece entrance hole and the first hole that members and guests see upon driving down the hill into the club. It is an unnerving par 3 over water to a wide and heavily contoured green. While any shot over water will test your nerves, the real challenge on this hole comes on the undulating putting surface where a shot played to the right side of the green can easily result in a three-putt.

The third hole underwent a renovation in 2007 following a massive windstorm that swept across western Washington in December 2006. The storm toppled 50 trees and destroyed the tees on the third hole. The club decided to renovate the entire hole except for the extremely interesting green surface. The tees were raised and leveled; the stairs and edges were removed to create a clear aesthetic; and the fairway was raised to improve drainage. The remaining storm-damaged poplars were removed from the roadside and finally the bunkers were rebuilt to restore their shape and improve playability. The result was a hole in which the members take great pride. It completes "The Loop" of the first three holes that return to the clubhouse and sets the stage for the challenges ahead.

Overlake's history on its current site dates back to 1927, when Francis L. James designed the 6,500-yard golf course, which evolved into the current design of the course completed in 1953 by the legendary A.V. Macan. Evolving with its classic history, Overlake has one of the youngest memberships in the Pacific Northwest and offers a modern, full menu of activities, including golf, aquatics, tennis, and a very active social calendar.

Photograph courtesy of Overlake Golf and Country Club

SAHALEE COUNTRY CLUB
South Course

9 HOLE

PAR 3 ◆ 213 YARDS

Sammamish, WA
425.868.8800
www.sahalee.com

On almost every hole in the towering forest you are reminded of Sahalee Country Club's original mission: to create a golf course capable of hosting a major championship. It is never more apparent than when stepping on the tee of the South Course's gracious and greedy ninth hole. The distance from the back tee, where the pros played it in the 1998 PGA Championship, is a healthy 213 yards; a par 3 that takes no prisoners and demands nothing less than total commitment.

There is simply no bailout. You either hit the green with your tee shot or find a placid pond that runs in front and left of the green. Consider playing right, away from the water, and nasty bunkers wait on the right-front of the hole. No matter where the pin is placed, the best play is to the middle of the green—if you can hit it that far and straight. Getting on the green doesn't mean the challenge is over, however. Subtle mounds running both front and back of the putting surface often demand a putt that can swing four or five feet on its way to the hole.

The club opened in 1969, a product of both designer Ted Robinson's vision and the founders' mission to take full advantage of the club's site on the Sammamish Plateau east of Seattle. Sahalee, which means "high heavenly ground," didn't stop with getting the PGA. It held the NEC World Championship in 2002 and the US Senior Open in 2010, all the while supporting amateur golf with its annual Sahalee Players Championship and the Edean Ihlanfeldt Invitational for women collegiate players.

Photograph by Rob Perry

SEATTLE GOLF CLUB

PAR 3 ◆ 165 YARDS

Seattle, WA
206.363.8811
www.seattlegolfclub.com

Enchanted is the place where the great Bobby Jones and President William Howard Taft played golf; where Jack Nicklaus helped the US demolish Britain and Ireland in a Walker Cup; and where the par-3 11th hole can look more like Augusta National than Augusta National. Its 100th birthday in the rearview mirror, Seattle Golf Club has loyal members who work arduously to retain "respect for tradition." And so it is, with a Swiss chalet-style clubhouse that looks like it did when Taft was there but works so much better, and with the enduring golf course overlooking Seattle's Highlands.

The 11th hole, not far from the clubhouse, is a members' favorite. It is a delicate hole, much like the 12th at Augusta, an all or nothing-at-all par 3. From the most used tee, the length is 165 yards, but it can vary from less than 100 yards to more than 200. For average players, the concern is making it over the lake in front of the hole. They'd just as soon have the pin as far from the water as it can be. Good players fear the back half of a severe two-tiered green, for anything that lands short or spins back leaves a very difficult two-putt to the back pin position.

Seattle Golf Club is different. It hosts only amateur events, and in selecting new members it is more about character than cash flow. It didn't raze its old clubhouse, but rather renovated it. In the 1990s when Arnold Palmer's design company suggested rerouting the 10th hole to the 11th green, changing the approach angle and losing the beautiful framing of the hole as it exists today, the members wouldn't have it, respecting tradition. They always do.

Photograph by Rob Perry

WINE VALLEY

Golf Club

14 HOLE

PAR 3 ◆ 160 YARDS

Walla Walla, WA
877.333.9842
www.winevalleygolfclub.com

At Wine Valley Golf Club, you are unmistakably in the tawny, windswept wheat fields of eastern Washington, yet the course's design is straight out of the British Isles, and the area's overriding allure of the nearly 100 wineries is absolutely French. Indeed, it was a French farmer who, long ago, planted a runaway Italian onion on the fertile landscape that would eventually turn into the famed Walla Walla sweet. As the 21st century unfolded and wine approached wheat as the area's number one crop, the need for a top-notch golf course emerged.

Wine Valley Golf Club is the design of Dan Hixson, a former club pro from Portland who was praised for his first design, Bandon Crossings on the Oregon Coast. The 14th hole at Wine Valley is the shortest and—according to handicap rankings—easiest on the course. It looks simple enough, even from the back-tee distance of 160 yards, and the second largest green on the course is relatively easy to hit. The good news is you're on the green. The bad news? You're on the green.

There are actually three greens in one that blend together to create an interesting challenge. Bunkers front and back leave one of the few forced carries on the course, appropriate for such a short hole and such a big green. But putting from one section of the green to another can be taxing and an invitation to a three- or four-putt. The most difficult pin placement is a small shelf in the top right corner of the green.

Wine Valley is a wonderful design and so at home in its vast, rolling landscape. The bunkers are large and deep. They fit the prevailing terrain and are filled with dark, indigenous sand.

Photograph by Brent Stewart

YAKIMA COUNTRY CLUB

PAR 3 ◆ 165 YARDS

Yakima, WA
509.452.2266
www.yakimacountryclub.org

Standing on the 17th green at Yakima Country Club presents golfers with a great view of the surrounding landscape on the horizon: Mount Adams, Mount Rainier, the entire front nine below in the valley, and Union Gap beyond.

This is a beautiful par 3 and part of a very difficult finish, where golfers face daunting golf shots on the par-4 16th, the par-3 17th, and the par-5 18th. Many Yakima tournaments are decided in the last three holes. Hole 17 acts as the swing hole, where leaders fall back with bad shots and followers catch up in glory.

Four different tee boxes give a variety of distances and angles to the green, which has two tiers and a narrow front and a pear-shaped back, offering many challenging pin placements. While the front tier can be attacked more easily, short shots roll down a steep-faced grass hill and long shots go into a bunker that forces a downhill trap shot.

If all that weren't enough, the trap that sits in front of the back-left side of the green catches many golf balls seemingly going at the pin, only to fall short. The view from hole 17 of the Yakima Valley and Union Gap is as informative as it is inspirational, for as wise members know and never forget, "all putts go to the Gap."

Photograph by Ronald Warninger

Tetherow Golf Club, page 121

Gearhart Golf Links, page 91

OREGON

Sandpines Golf Links, page 95

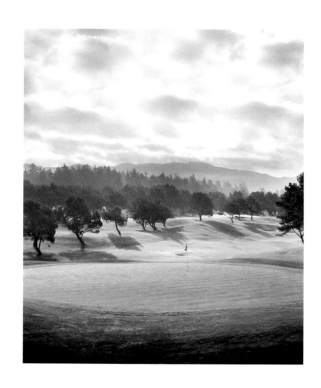

GEARHART
Golf Links

PAR 5 ◆ 585 YARDS

Gearhart, OR
503.738.3538
www.gearhartgolflinks.com

For the first 17 holes of Gearhart Golf Links, the more than 100-year-old course is amiable and genteel, with inviting fairways and eye-pleasing dunescapes. A scattering of short par 4s, sprinkled with three par 3s—two long and one short—and two par 5s on the property's edge lead you around this coastal gem. Standing on the tee of the 18th hole, you are suddenly faced with one of the biggest of "big boy" holes. The finishing hole is long, demanding two huge shots just to get in sight of the green and a third shot up left to an elevated green. It's also narrow, out-of-bounds on the left, with a fairway that heaves with rolling mounds like the nearby Pacific Ocean. The green itself is no haven either, sloping severely from back-left to front-right. If you're against the wind—which is almost a certainty in the summer—forget about it.

The saving grace is the pure beauty of the hole and the sight of the beach-style clubhouse, replete with a McMenamins pub, behind the green. Golf itself boasts a long and mythical residency in Gearhart, appearing almost from the moment nails were being pounded into boards to build Gearhart's first home. Legend has it that Gearhart began life in about 1888, starting out as three holes of true links-style golf, making it the oldest course in the Northwest and arguably in the western United States.

Founded by Robert Livingstone, who was also the president of Waverley Country Club in Portland, the golf course has been molded and polished over the years by Marshall Kinney, Olympic gold medal golfer and US Amateur champion H. Chandler Egan, and Oregon architect William G. Robinson. To this day, the course retains that classic links-style flavor with a hint of traditional Northwest design features.

Photographs by Don Frank

THE RESERVE VINEYARDS AND GOLF CLUB

North Course

PAR 5 ◆ 501 YARDS

Aloha, OR
503.649.8191
www.reservegolf.com

Situated in the heart of Oregon's wine country, The Reserve Vineyards and Golf Club is valued as much for the competitive golf it has seen as the verdant scenery it embraces. Although relatively new, the course has already been the site of Peter Jacobsen's Fred Meyer Challenge as well as one of the major events on the PGA's Champions Tour, the Jeld-Wen Tradition. Many of golf's greatest players, including Phil Mickelson, Jack Nicklaus, Arnold Palmer, and Annika Sorenstam have walked its fairways.

There are two wonderful 18-hole courses at The Reserve that alternate between public and private use. The 18th hole on the North Course is a classic risk/reward finishing hole with a lake at the green's right-front edge, providing grief for some and glory for others. It is a stunning finish to a round of golf, with the chateau-like clubhouse reflecting in the water. The championship tees sit at just over 500 yards, encouraging better players to go for the green in two. Other less talented, but often more successful, players will choose to lay up in front of the green and pitch a shot that can net an opportunity for birdie, or certainly a par.

North Course designer Bob Cupp is also noted for his work at Crosswater and Pumpkin Ridge. Providing dramatic contrast to the John Fought-designed South Course, which is pure Willamette Valley in character, the North Course is like playing among Oregon's celebrated coastal dunes.

Photograph courtesy of The Reserve Vineyards and Golf Club

SANDPINES
Golf Links

PAR 5 ◆ 519 YARDS

Florence, OR
800.917.4653
www.sandpines.com

Designed by the famed "US Open doctor" Rees Jones, Sandpines Golf Links was declared the best new public course in the country when it opened in 1993. Sculpted through dunes that are adjacent to the Oregon Dunes National Recreation Area, Sandpines is not just a stopover on the way to Bandon Dunes, but a worthy destination of its own. The front nine is out of North Carolina, boasting tall pines and small lakes, while the inward nine is out of Scotland, with wind and holes weaving among massive dunes. It all comes together—sand and water—for the final three holes, perhaps the best three finishing holes in the state of Oregon.

As the back nine emerges from the dunes, everything converges around a large lake viewed from the clubhouse. The 16th hole is a short, downhill, drivable par 4 that sits next to the lake, setting the stage for a rugged, into-the-wind and over-the-water par 3. Watching golfers finish their rounds while taking in the spectacular views from the deck of its beautiful 9,000-square-foot clubhouse is a Sandpines specialty. But the real fun is the 18th hole, where all that was lost on the 17th can be regained with a birdie, or perhaps even an eagle.

Playing downwind, the par 5 can be reached in two if the drive stays dry left and misses bunkers on the right. And if the second shot can similarly avoid water left, in most cases it can be drawn into a green that has bunkers toward the back of the hole. This hole especially is risk/reward, with the emphasis on reward.

Photograph by Patrick Drickey

TETHEROW
Golf Club

13 HOLE

PAR 5 ◆ 588 YARDS

Bend, OR
541.388.2582
www.tetherow.com

At times, playing Tetherow is like playing John Wayne or the Lone Ranger in an old Western movie. With the tee shot on the 13th hole being partially blind, you survey the glorious high-desert landscape looking for some direction, perhaps a puff of smoke in the distance. Coming back to reality, the caddy's tip is to aim at Broken Top Mountain. So much for the movies, but what a fascinating place to play golf.

Two large pines mark the left side of this wide fairway, but danger lurks for the longer hitters as they can hit through the fairway and into the brush or a deceptive bunker. The second shot on this 588-yard par 5, a layup for most, should be well short of the green since there is no need to flirt with the water.

Central Oregon basalt is on full display in the middle of the hole while providing a chute to play through. A snakelike bunker extends down the left creating one of the most dramatic snapshots on the course.

Members know that you can use the contours on the right to feed the ball to the center of the green. The back section of the green runs away from the player potentially ending in disaster.

Photograph by Jonathan Kingston

COLUMBIA EDGEWATER
Country Club

PAR 4 ◆ 420 YARDS

Portland, OR
503.285.3676
www.cecc.com

The definition of a classic is: "something judged over a period of time to be of the highest quality." The green on the eighth hole at Columbia Edgewater Country Club is certainly a classic, but it's also an original, having been designed by the famed A.V. Macan in 1925. It was Macan, a championship player who lost only two strokes on his handicap after losing his foot in World War I, who implemented the same strategic simplicity in the Northwest that Alister MacKenzie did in California. Columbia Edgewater has its own grand history, having been 25 times the site of an LPGA tour event and also a frequent and challenging host to the Oregon Open and, before that, the Portland Open. Annika Sorenstam, twice a winner at Columbia Edgewater, called the greens the best she'd ever played.

The eighth hole is a subtle but strong par 4, with a hidden lake adjacent to the fairway that a long, errant shot can uncover. The best drives are to the left side of the fairway, but the real challenge is in the tri-level green that has seen its fair share of three putts.

Neighboring the largest river in the Pacific Northwest on Portland's Marine Drive, Columbia Edgewater is celebrated for its wonderful year-round playing conditions, its bevy of single-digit handicap members, and the Short Game Practice Facility and par-3 Mason Course designed by former head professional and nationally accredited designer Dan Hixson and the legendary Bunny Mason.

As golf looks to its past to better prepare for its future, Macan's approach is being revived in many circles. He placed hazards less to penalize players than to challenge low handicappers. Another Macan trait was an uncanny ability to design greens with drainage suitable for the Northwest's wet climate—something that is still showcased today at Columbia Edgewater.

Photograph by Dave Wilson

CREEKSIDE
Golf Club

PAR 4 ◆ 417 YARDS

Salem, OR
503.363.4653
www.golfcreekside.com

The pastoral pleasure of Oregon's Willamette Valley serves as an appropriate and beautiful backdrop for Creekside Golf Club in Salem. Designed in the early 1990s by the state's most popular golfer, Peter Jacobsen, Creekside is a serious golf course: It's been host to the Oregon Open, the Oregon Amateur, and the 2011 and 2012 NAIA National Championships as well as qualifying for the U.S. Senior Open. The fifth hole, a 417-yard par 4 from the back tees, is the most beautiful hole on the course and is sure to be the most photographed.

A wide fairway bunkered strategically on both sides makes a good drive essential because anything less means a layup short of Battle Creek, which bisects the fairway and then swings precariously around the right edge of the green. Indeed, there are five fairway bunkers on the fifth, three to the left side and two to the right. The tee shot presents a point of no return. Find a bunker and you can't get over the creek; lay up short of the fairway bunkers and you can't get there either. To make matters more challenging, there is a bunker to the left side of a green that stealthily slopes away.

The challenge at Creekside often comes down to an ability to read and putt the greens—once you get to them, of course. Even though it is a parkland golf course in a luscious setting, Creekside shows Jacobsen's love for links-style golf and has touches of both the ground and aerial games.

Photograph by Ean Perkins

EUGENE
Country Club

PAR 4 ◆ 440 YARDS

Eugene, OR
541.345.0181
www.eugenecountryclub.com

The magnificent firs that stand sentinel at Eugene Country Club, for decades the highest-ranked course in the Pacific Northwest, are considered hallowed halls. In the 1960s, although already the site of LPGA tour events, Eugene undertook an ambitious renovation by the renowned Robert Trent Jones Sr. To enable play to continue during construction and to limit removal of the trees, Jones built greens where tees once were, and tees where greens were. The result was a dramatic old course with towering trees and new, diabolical green complexes.

Out there among the cathedral of firs and cedars is a testy par 4, the 440-yard 15th. Often the decider in match play, it's a hole demanding a well-struck and well-placed drive to escape a long line of trees on the left side of the fairway. The green is at the end of a sharp dogleg left and is obscured from the tee shot with anything hit left or short.

The telltale second shot is over a swale and among a series of bunkers to a green that runs perpendicular to the fairway. Any approach short is in a bunker or rolling down into the swale. The best bailout is left of the green, but go too far and there is yet another bunker with which to contend. The green—Stimpmeters often read 13 or more at Eugene—slopes left to right.

Photograph by John R. Johnson

PORTLAND
Golf Club

HOLE 11

PAR 4 ◆ 370 YARDS

Portland, OR
503.292.2651
www.portlandgolfclub.com

Portland Golf Club has so much history and cache that they simply call the 11th the "Mallard Hole." The delicate par 4 can require a blind approach to an elevated and severely sloping back-to-front green. To start with, the tee shot must carry Junor Lake to even get to an uphill landing area. The lake has its own story, created in 1926 to add attractiveness and sportiness to the course as well as impounding water from Woods Creek that would be used for irrigation—Portland Golf Club was the first club in the state to water its fairways.

While even the most skilled putter can be intimidated by the green, there was a stretch in the '50s and '60s when Billy Casper, a three-time Portland Open champion, made seven birdies in eight tries. It's just one of many stories at a storied club that has seen the likes of Ben Hogan, Peter Jacobsen, Bobby Jones, Nancy Lopez, Cary Middlecoff, Byron Nelson, Jack Nicklaus, Greg Norman, Arnold Palmer, Gary Player, Sam Snead, Payne Stewart, Lee Trevino, and Kathy Whitworth grace its fairways. Hogan won the 1946 PGA Championship at Portland Golf Club and led the US to a sweep of the Brits in the 1947 Ryder Cup there. In 1945, Hogan shot 65-69-63-64 to win the Portland Open. The 63—tied by Middlecoff at the Western Open—stands to this day as the course record. More recently, Ben Crane, a PGA Tour winner, learned the game at Portland Golf Club as a third-generation member. And the Mallard Hole? It still ranks as a great test of skill, as well as a sanctuary for wild birds.

Photograph courtesy of Portland Golf Club

PUMPKIN RIDGE

Ghost Creek Golf Club

PAR 4 ◆ 454 YARDS

North Plains, OR
503.647.9977
www.pumpkinridge.com

Like a fine symphony production, the Ghost Creek course at Pumpkin Ridge Golf Club reaches a memorable crescendo. Sometimes, too memorable.

Pumpkin Ridge is a splendid, sprawling golf complex in the foothills west of Portland that has been host to a US Amateur—won by Tiger Woods—two US Women's Opens, a US Women's Amateur, a Nike Tour championship won by David Duval, and several Safeway Classics. The scenic setting of agricultural fields framed by imposing evergreens was so perfect that designer Bob Cupp campaigned to build two courses, not just one.

The 18th hole at Ghost Creek—the public access course—is so demanding that it can affect how you play the 17th hole; a short, drivable par 4 that can offer a birdie if you're courageous enough to go after it. Yet the difficulty of the 18th hole, a 454-yard par 4, might give pause to golfers thinking about taking a risk on the 17th.

The 18th is clearly a catch-up hole. It demands a long, straight drive through the opening between the two towering firs while avoiding a creek on the right side of the fairway. Your second shot is a long one to the green—a lake awaits to swallow balls that miss short or a little to the right.

The green has a spine running right to left to further complicate matters. Many players try to stay a little left of center coming into the green, but can't hit too far for fear of dumping the ball into a green-side collection area.

The 18th surround includes areas able to accomodate 10,000-plus spectators—a wise addition as there is always something to see on this spectacular finishing hole.

Photograph © D Squared Productions

THE RESORT AT THE MOUNTAIN
Pine Cone Nine

PAR 4 ◆ 426 YARDS

Welches, OR
503.622.3151
www.theresort.com

From the very beginning, you notice something special about this place on the shoulder of majestic Mount Hood. Like, on the very first hole, you step over a serious salmon working its way up what they affectionately call the Wee Burn. As it works its way down the left side of the first fairway on the Pine Cone Nine, Wee Burn—not the salmon—can become the big pain, a hazard pinching in the left side of the fairway as you try to avoid the bunker on the right side of the fairway.

While saving salmon has been a 10-year-long project, The Resort at The Mountain golf course has been there nearly as long as the mountain, debuting in 1928 as Oregon's first resort golf course. Over the years, the resort has added holes—it now has three nines—to become a haven for golfers in the summer and skiers in the winter. In one of his final projects, John Harbottle III added bunkers, like those on the first hole of Pine Cone, and made as much use of the Wee Burn—a tributary to the nearby Salmon River—as he could.

The key at the first is a drive that avoids the burn and the bunker, although there are those who can drive it over the bunker for a much shorter approach to a two-tiered green guarded on the left by a deep bunker. Only the bombers should apply, however, as it is 250 yards to clear the back of the fairway bunker, aided perhaps by the resort's 1,300-foot elevation, but probably not enough.

Photograph by Gary Randall

ROCK CREEK
Country Club

PAR 4 ◆ 395 YARDS

Portland, OR
503.645.1115
www.rockcreekcountryclub.com

The members at Rock Creek Country Club like to refer to their golf course as the best-kept secret in Portland. However, there is no secret about the beguiling 14th hole: Treat it with the respect it deserves, or perish. The choice is obvious from the tee of the 395-yard dogleg par 4. Either risk putting your tee shot out of bounds by trying to overpower the tall trees down the left side of the fairway and get a wedge to the green, or resign to play carefully to the middle of the fairway and be content with a medium-iron shot to the green. Any shot, from any distance, to the small, quick green is a challenging one.

The 14th is also the first of a series of demanding finishing holes. Next up is a par 3 that can stretch to over 190 yards. The tee shot must be played over water and around an ash tree that sits ominously in the pond. The 16th hole is another long

par 4, and the 17th is a par 5 with a creek in front of the green and little room for a layup shot.

Rock Creek has morphed into a course that is both welcoming and challenging, noted for its small, smooth, and fast greens, as well as tree-lined fairways that can bring down any errant shot. From the back tees, the course is a test, with a rating of 72.4 and a slope of 128. Located in a quiet, quaint neighborhood, Rock Creek has a grass driving range, dry-in-the-winter fairways, and isn't totally unhappy about remaining the best-kept secret in Portland.

Photographs by RCCC Photography

TETHEROW GOLF CLUB

6 HOLE

PAR 4 ◆ 424 YARDS

Bend, OR
541.388.2582
www.tetherow.com

The sixth hole at Tetherow Golf Club shows off the best of what the acclaimed course has to offer: stunning beauty and creative, challenging golf. The course's designer, David McLay Kidd, calls it one of the most enthralling holes he has created. It has become known as the anchor of Kidd's Corner, a daunting four holes starting at the third.

The elevated tees on the sixth offer stunning views of the surrounding landscape. But it is the decision-making that makes this hole so memorable. This is a true split-fairway, risk/reward hole. The lower left fairway skirts the water on the left and is guarded by a ridge of clumps and bunkers on the right, while the right fairway is comparatively generous but leaves a blind second shot. Members know that they can

play to the right fairway and still have a good opportunity to run their approach shot to the green, but first-time players find the approach shot intimidating.

The elevated green requires a deft touch to get near the pin. With three different tiers, getting close to the pin is a must when chasing birdie. The toughest pin is a nasty little section of the green front-right that can often frustrate the uninitiated. The back of the green slopes hard to the left, and any approach shot through the green leaves a daunting up and down.

It's a spectacular hole where the best decision might be to play it again and again.

Photograph by Jonathan Kingston

TUALATIN
Country Club

PAR 4 ◆ 422 YARDS

Tualatin, OR
503.692.1122
www.tualatincountryclub.com

Tualatin Country Club is the fourth-oldest club in Oregon. The course was originally designed in 1912 by H. Chandler Egan, a US Amateur champion and winner of a silver medal in the only Olympics to have golf. He added to his acclaim with his renovation of Pebble Beach in 1929—with Alister MacKenzie—and his design of more than 20 golf courses, mainly in the Northwest. When John Fought, the 1977 US Amateur champion and former club member, returned to renovate Tualatin Country Club in 1991, the course certainly had a past worth preserving.

While country clubs are often thought of as elitist, Tualatin Country Club was established in response to the exclusionary nature of others. In the early 1900s, Jewish people were not allowed at other Oregon private clubs, so they built Tualatin on more than 100 acres of farmland on the outskirts of Portland, near a local train line. Its membership has included many prominent Portland businessmen and professionals, including Julius Meier of Meier & Frank department stores, who later

became Oregon's governor. It wasn't until the 1960s that non-Jewish members joined the club. Tualatin retains a special relationship with two other Northwest Jewish-founded clubs: Glendale Country Club in Bellevue, Washington, and Richmond Country Club in British Columbia.

Tualatin's golf course, with small greens and diabolical bunkering, holds its own in high level competitions, including hosting eight Oregon State Amateur Championships and numerous USGA and PNW PGA events. The finishing hole is a difficult, long par 4 that requires the use of a driver off the tee, aimed right of center to avoid a left-side fairway bunker. From there, a mid-iron shot to the green must carry a pond on the right edge of the green, while also avoiding bunkers behind and to the left. The large multitiered green offers many difficult pin locations and is a great challenge as you complete your round.

Photographs courtesy of Tualatin Country Club

WILDHORSE
Golf Course

18 HOLE

PAR 4 ◆ 463 YARDS

Pendleton, OR
800.654.9453
www.wildhorseresort.com

Whether in a friendly match or with the Senior Oregon Open Invitational title at stake, no lead is safe if you have not yet faced the 18th hole at Wildhorse Golf Course. In fact, water along the right side of the fairway can commandeer shots not once, but twice, making a long straight drive necessary to have a chance at par. Wildhorse, a beautifully manicured links-style layout, is located in the high desert near Pendleton. Designed in the 1990s by John Steidel, it was the first modern tribal golf course in the Northwest, and it builds to a terrific finish.

For most of the way, undulating, quick greens protect par at the scenic Wildhorse course. But on the 18th, getting to the green is the challenge. The hole measures 474 yards from the gold tees with out-of-bounds left and water coming into play about 240 yards off the tee to the right. As you move up sets of tees, the water at right looms for everyone. The second shot on the 18th still must contend with it, but also with a bunker on the left. There are reasons to lay up, but the area 30 yards short of the green actually narrows a bit.

The course sits next to the Wildhorse Resort & Casino, a destination so popular that the Confederated Tribes of the Umatilla Indian Reservation—the Cayuse, the Umatilla, and the Walla Walla—have added a 10-story, 202 luxury room hotel, as well as a five-screen cinema, while at the same time doubling the size of its gaming floor. The course is well worth playing; at Wildhorse, the fun does not stop at the 18th hole.

Photograph by Ric Walters, Studio 421

OREGON GOLF CLUB 12^{HOLE}

PAR 3 ♦ 189 YARDS

West Linn, OR
503.650.6900
www.oregongolfclub.com

Peter Jacobsen is the face of golf in Oregon; a Portland native who insists on living there even though on tour and while other pros from northern climes move to Arizona and Florida. In the early '90s, Jacobsen designed Oregon Golf Club in the sprawling hills above the Willamette River, so near and yet so far from downtown Portland. He wanted to embrace the Oregon of his youth and the great courses of his travels, especially those in Scotland. His 7,052-yard course is sculpted from an expansive swath of farmland in the shadows of the Cascade Mountains.

While Jacobsen cleverly blended the best of Scotland and Oregon, there are always the reminders of Augusta National, from the Oregon Golf Club logo—whose inspiration Jacobsen allegedly drew from the restroom wallpaper at Augusta—to the hundreds of roses on the par-3 12th that remind some of the sixth hole at Augusta.

The 12th is a beautiful but devilish hole, with its narrow green perched on a hillside. Any shot to the green either makes it or doesn't—there is no in-between.

Still it is the beauty and not the beast that you remember. It was the favorite hole of club founder Tadamasa Ohno, who is remembered with a plaque on the hole's set of silver tees. Along with the thousands of roses on the grounds, there are stunning views of Mount Hood, Mount Adams, and Mount St. Helens. Oregon Golf Club was the home of the Fred Meyer Challenge and also served as the site of the NCAA women's championship in 1994, and both the Oregon Amateur and Oregon Open.

Photograph © D Squared Productions

TETHEROW GOLF CLUB

PAR 3 ◆ 182 YARDS

Bend, OR
541.388.2582
www.tetherow.com

The use of the phrase "signature hole" is despised by most golf course architects, who would rather be judged on the totality of their work rather than the compelling look of one hole. But some holes stand alone. Renowned architect David McLay Kidd, who did the first golf course at Bandon Dunes as well as the Castle Course at St. Andrews, Scotland, doesn't mind the term "cover-girl hole," and if Tetherow has one, it is the 17th.

The 182-yard hole sits down in a pumice quarry and holds one of the smallest greens Kidd has ever built, measuring less than 3,000 square feet. The exposed pumice throughout the hole is the real eye-catcher, providing an intimidating carry off the tee. The giant backboard left and long of this green is the true target, allowing the ball to feed close to almost any pin position. The fun of this hole is watching what happens after the ball lands, as the friendly contours provide exciting finishes. Avoid, if you can, the bunker on the right, for it is deep and gnarly and can provide some unruly lies.

Many have called this the best inland hole in Oregon, and it definitely lives up to the hype. The 17th is Tetherow's true "cover-girl."

Photograph by Jonathan Kingston

WAVERLEY
Country Club

PAR 3 ◆ 130 YARDS

Portland, OR
503.654.6521
www.waverley.cc

At Waverley Country Club it has always been about the total experience. So it is not surprising that the venerable venue should dwell on its ninth hole, a mere 130-yard par 3. Taking the tee at the ninth, there lies before you the magnificent clubhouse and lawns sprawling down to the edge of the Willamette River. But it is best that your attention is not lost in the euphoria of the scene and the length of the hole, for painted across the front of the square green is a bunker that is more of a moat than a simple sand trap. Find the bunker and lose all thoughts of a birdie or even par.

While the 1896-founded Waverley is about history—six USGA championships, including Tiger Woods' third of three junior titles—it has enjoyed a rigorous update at the hands of Gil Hanse, designer of the 2016 Olympic Games' course in Rio de Janeiro. A relative unknown at the time, Hanse was selected by the folks at Waverley from an esteemed field that included David McLay Kidd, Tom Doak, and Tom Fazio. The renovation by Hanse in 2010 included the removal of many trees, occasionally replacing them with fairway bunkers. The tree removal improved growing conditions, opened up views of the river, and changed the Waverley mantra of "keep the ball between the trees."

Hanse touched every hole on the course, always aware of Waverley's history for serving as "the center of the golf universe in Oregon since 1896" while adding elements of decision-making. Waverley, as typified by the ninth hole, is a course to be enjoyed, not feared, now more than ever.

Photograph by Jim Gibbons

Sun Valley, page 129

Coeur d'Alene Golf Resort, page 137

IDAHO

Whitetail Club, page 135

BANBURY
Golf Course

PAR 5 ◆ 544 YARDS

Eagle, ID
208.939.3600
www.banburygolf.com

Built in the watery wilderness of the south channel of the Boise River, BanBury Golf Course is the paramount creation of the late John Harbottle III. Water comes into play on all 18 holes, and it was Harbottle's challenge to make the water as strategic as it was beautiful. He forged a track that is annually voted among Idaho's best; a track designed to look more difficult than it is while still maintaining its stirring challenges. The stretch of holes starting at the eighth and ending at the 14th is known by locals as Eagle's Revenge. Perhaps pivotal is the 544-yard 12th, a risk/reward hole for very few and a darn-hard, three-shot par 5 for the rest.

To say water comes into play is an understatement. A creek crosses the fairway twice, once in front of the tee and again about 290 yards from the back tees and 250 from the mortal tees. A few big-hitters can attempt to drive the second creek, a play that requires a high draw over some trees. For the rest there is a 240-yard layup shot, setting up a second shot that must be short of bunkers to the right side of the fairway about 100 yards from a green that slopes from back-left to front-right.

Following Eagle's Revenge are a few birdie holes, including the go-for-it par-5 18th, where in 2005 Morgan Pressel, the 17-year-old who lost to an improbable chip-in at the US Open one month prior, saw her dreams of winning the US Junior Girls end when she plunked one in the lake at the 18th.

Photograph courtesy of BanBury Golf Course

SUN VALLEY
White Clouds Nine

5 HOLE

PAR 5 ◆ 637 YARDS

Sun Valley, ID
208.622.2251
www.sunvalley.com/golf

When standing atop the White Clouds Nine at Sun Valley, your eye captures a stunning 360-degree view of the Wood River Valley, encompassing Bald Mountain, Dollar Mountain, the Pioneer Mountains, Angel's Perch, Devil's Bedstead, and the home of Ernest Hemingway. Approaching the fifth tee box, golfers first notice the words of the Sun Valley Resort owner inscribed on a stone marker: "This is not all about golf."

White Clouds—a nine-hole addition to the Sun Valley Resort golf scene that opened in 2008—reaches dramatically from one plateau to another; nine holes with breathtaking views and memorable shots. It is links-style golf because it has few trees and lots of bunkers, and is as fun as it is difficult, as fascinating as it is frustrating.

The course begins its ascent on the second hole with a par 3 hanging over the gorge, and then a short par 4 that has as much risk as there is reward. Then comes the first of back-to-back par 5s, climaxed with the fiendish fifth that is generally best managed rather than conquered. First of all, it can play more than 600 yards. At this point and at that altitude, you might think you need a sherpa rather than a golf cart. The tee shot should avoid anything left, as should the second shot; if hit right and long enough it will funnel down toward a green that is a reverse tier and slopes from front to back. As memorable as the hole is, the location and especially the views are what you really remember—just as the owner, the late R. Earl Holding, hoped you would when he added that plaque.

Photographs courtesy of Sun Valley

CIRCLING RAVEN
Golf Club

PAR 4 ◆ 386 YARDS

Worley, ID
800.523.2464
www.circlingraven.com

The accolades—best public course in Idaho, best tribal course in America, among others—are one thing. But it is the sensation of playing Circling Raven Golf Club, seemingly alone among more than 600 acres, which lingers. From many of the holes, no other people, houses, or flags are visible. The eighth hole, called Snow on the Mountain, is certainly a signature, but at Circling Raven every hole seems worthy of that designation.

Once you've observed the snow on the mountain, next comes a tee shot over the deep, yawning, and sizeable wetlands that extend down the right side of the hole. Down the left side are trees, pine straw, and a slope to avoid. A drive slightly left of center seems prudent, avoiding a fairway bunker on the right, but really the fun has only just begun. The approach into the smallest green on the course must avoid a bunker to the right and more wetlands down the slope behind the green. Beware of a sucker pin right, tucked behind the bunker in a very small landing area.

The Coeur d'Alene tribe was true to its traditions and vision with the development of Circling Raven. The tribe provided 620 acres for the golf course to guarantee Mother Nature's place in the experience. Only 110 of those acres are developed; the rest left as wetlands, woodlands, and Palouse grasslands. Among the architects to make course proposals was Jack Nicklaus, who wanted to locate the course across the highway from the casino, away from the wetlands and old railroad tracks and bridges. Florida architect Gene Bates chose the road less traveled, calling for a course that would use the wetlands and the railroad trestles and be as interesting as the site itself. Bates got the job, and the rest is remarkable history.

Photograph by John R. Johnson

SUN VALLEY
Trail Creek Course

14 HOLE

PAR 4 ◆ 382 YARDS

Sun Valley, ID
208.622.2251
www.sunvalley.com/golf

One of Idaho's most acclaimed layouts, the Trail Creek course at Sun Valley bridges a golf gap between classic and modern. The Robert Trent Jones Jr. design of the '80s honors the natural setting of one of America's original resorts. With the famous ski slopes—the first chairlift was developed here in the 1930s—looking on from above, the Trail Creek course occupies the valley below, winding its way through trees and across a stream. The 14th hole is a short par 4—382 yards from the championship tees—that has a beautiful stairstep of bunkers along the left side of the hole.

The key is to keep your drive right without being too friendly with a stand of trees or, beyond them, out-of-bounds markers.

Otherwise a shot from the left must find its way over that seductive string of bunkers, which can produce long, uphill sand shots to the green. Once there, the green offers a large and relatively flat surface, sloping slightly from back to front, a reward for getting there in the first place.

Sun Valley has been recognized by *Golf Digest* as one of the top 75 resort courses in North America. The Jones design artistically follows the creek to supply a full complement of shots to best avoid water and bunkers. The course crosses the creek seven times in the first nine holes alone.

Photograph courtesy of Sun Valley

WHITETAIL CLUB

PAR 4 ◆ 390 YARDS

McCall, ID
208.630.0211
www.whitetailclub.com

Whitetail Club's championship golf course was designed by two-time US Open Champion Andy North and Roger Packard, and has consistently been named a top course in the western United States by *Golf Digest* and *Golfweek* magazines. Many holes on the course wind through the towering ponderosa pines demanding control off the tee. The finishing holes provide open, water-laced meadows with spectacular views of Long Valley.

The 11th hole comes at a strategic time in a stretch of the most demanding holes on the course. After holing out on the difficult 10th, golfers proceed to the 11th, where they'll find the straightaway par 4. The 11th hole features an elevated tee with views of Boulder Mountain framed by towering ponderosa pines. Length is not a priority in playing the hole well. At 365 yards from the middle tees, a well-struck tee shot through the corridor of pines will come to rest at the bottom of the valley. From that point, a short iron will likely be the club of choice. Though the second shot is not long, distance and direction are priorities in making par or birdie. The small, elevated green is heavily guarded by four deep bunkers just waiting to gobble up any ball left short. One of the more level greens on the course and receptive to holing putts, the 11th can be your friend if you've made it to the green safely.

Photograph courtesy of Whitetail Club

COEUR D'ALENE
Golf Resort

PAR 3 ◆ 175 YARDS

Coeur d'Alene, ID
208.667.4653
www.cdaresort.com

For those who have played there and those who haven't but yearn to, the 14th at Coeur d'Alene Golf Resort remains one of the world's most photographed and best-known golf holes. Picture them: the 16th at Cypress Point, the 18th at Pebble Beach, the 13th at Augusta National, the 18th at St. Andrews, the 17th at TPC Sawgrass, all upholding the icon definition as "an object of uncritical devotion." And the 14th at Coeur d'Alene.

It began with a sudden fit of inspiration; the owner of the industrial property walking his dog, gazing out at a tugboat towing a nearly round raft of logs on Lake Coeur d'Alene. He asked himself, and his dog, "Why couldn't that be a green?" Duane Hagadone spent three times what any other green has cost to build the floating green, but most difficult was convincing his architect, Scott Miller, to even attempt it. The green, engineered with foam-filled concrete beams and an electronically controlled cable system, can be moved to or away from shore, less than 100 yards

and more than 200 yards, but in any event the hole requires a respectable shot to the massive, 15,000-square-foot green replete with bunkers fore and aft. A small boat named *Putter* takes you to the green. Those who make par get a certificate celebrating the fact, while those who end up in the water—more than half the first tries do—get to do it again.

The floating green isn't the only extravaganza at Coeur d'Alene. A mahogany boat brings you to the course where there is a complimentary massage before you play. And there's more: forecaddies who take on-course service to an entirely new level, luxurious custom carts, views of the lake from nearly every hole, and finely manicured bent grass tees and fairways. Indeed, the posh course ensures that you feel thoroughly pampered, utterly spoiled, and simply lucky to enjoy such a unique golf experience.

Photograph by Joel Riner, Quicksilver Studios

THE GOLF CLUB
at Black Rock

PAR 3 ◆ 155 YARDS

Coeur d'Alene, ID
208.676.8999
www.blackrockidaho.com

The par-3 13th hole at The Golf Club at Black Rock is not the most difficult hole on the course, although standing on the tee will cause even the best of player to lose focus. The 155-yard hole is gloriously draped with five 40-foot waterfalls cascading down huge black rocks left of the green. If that isn't enough, large boulders and a lone pine tree frame the right side of the hole. Stunning views of boat traffic on Lake Coeur d'Alene serve as an overall backdrop.

The hole provides two challenges to the player: Pick the right club from the elevated tee and don't get wrapped up in the surroundings. Named the best new private course in America by *Golf Digest* in 2003, Black Rock is an aesthetic masterpiece; a 7,135-yard mountain course crafted by designer and architect Jim Engh. It is a scenic trail of bent grass fairways and greens navigating through native basalt rock formations overlooking the lake.

With tightly mowed fairways and a few bowl-shaped greens, delicate and creative shot-making is of the highest order. Even though it is a relatively late addition to the rankings, Black Rock has consistently been among *Golf Digest's* top 100 courses in America.

Photograph courtesy of The Golf Club at Black Rock

HUNTSMAN SPRINGS

PAR 3 ◆ 164 YARDS

Driggs, ID
208.354.9660
www.huntsmansprings.com

Huntsman Springs, a masterful blending of water and sand in the shadow of three mountain ranges, has been labeled by its designer, David McLay Kidd, as the "the pinnacle of my career." The drop-dead beauty of the 11th hole is matched only by the hole itself, a stern par 3 where club selection is paramount.

You need a swing that will get you pin high from tee boxes ranging from less than 100 yards to almost 200; a club that will carry the pond in front of the hole and hopefully find the proper section of a green that is bisected front to back by a ridge. Get on the wrong side of the ridge, and three putts can quickly curb the euphoria of the moment. If the pin is on the left, a shot that catches that section can follow a funnel effect to the hole, where birdies and even aces are possible.

Huntsman Springs' design, included on many new best course lists, matches its mountains—no small achievement in this part of the country. Kidd moved four million cubic yards of sand and gravel to create the humps and bumps of a links course, and corralled the snow runoff to add numerous water hazards. Everywhere there are touches of Old World authenticity thanks to the wavy fescue grasses that surround the bunkers.

Photograph by Laurence Lambrecht

Publishing Team

PUBLISHER: Brian G. Carabet
PUBLISHER: John A. Shand
ASSOCIATE PUBLISHER: Marc Zurba
ART DIRECTOR: Emily A. Kattan
GRAPHIC DESIGNER: Mara Lane
EDITOR: Blaine Newnham
EDITOR: Megan Winkler
DIRECTOR OF BOOK DEVELOPMENT: Rosalie Z. Wilson
ADMINISTRATIVE COORDINATOR: Amanda Mathers

White Horse Golf Club, page 65

THE PANACHE COLLECTION

Dream Homes Series

An Exclusive Showcase of the Finest Architects, Designers and Builders

Carolinas, Chicago, Coastal California, Colorado, Deserts, Florida, Georgia, Los Angeles, Metro New York, Michigan, Minnesota, New England, New Jersey, Northern California, Ohio & Pennsylvania, Pacific Northwest, Philadelphia, South Florida, Southwest, Tennessee, Texas, Washington, D.C., Extraordinary Homes California

Spectacular Homes Series

An Exclusive Showcase of the Finest Interior Designers

California, Carolinas, Chicago, Colorado, Florida, Georgia, Heartland, London, Michigan, Minnesota, New England, Metro New York, Ohio & Pennsylvania, Pacific Northwest, Philadelphia, South Florida, Southwest, Tennessee, Texas, Toronto, Washington, D.C., Western Canada

Perspectives on Design Series

Design Philosophies Expressed by Leading Professionals

California, Carolinas, Chicago, Colorado, Florida, Georgia, Great Lakes, London, Minnesota, New England, New York, Pacific Northwest, South Florida, Southwest, Toronto, Western Canada

Art of Celebration Series

Inspiration and Ideas from Top Event Professionals

Chicago & the Greater Midwest, Colorado, Georgia, New England, New York, Northern California, South Florida, Southern California, Southern Style, Southwest, Toronto, Washington, D.C.

City by Design Series

An Architectural Perspective

Atlanta, Charlotte, Chicago, Dallas, Denver, New York, Orlando, Phoenix, San Francisco, Texas

Spectacular Wineries Series

A Captivating Tour of Established, Estate and Boutique Wineries

California's Central Coast, Napa Valley, New York, Ontario, Oregon, Sonoma County, Texas, Washington

Experience Series

The Most Interesting Attractions, Hotels, Restaurants, and Shops

Austin & the Hill Country, British Columbia, Thompson Okanagan

Interiors Series

Leading Designers Reveal Their Most Brilliant Spaces

Florida, Midwest, New York, Southeast, Washington, D.C.

Golf Series

The Most Scenic and Challenging Golf Holes

Arizona, Colorado, Ontario, Pacific Northwest, Southeast, Texas, Western Canada

Weddings Series

Captivating Destinations and Exceptional Resources Introduced by the Finest Event Planners

Southern California

Luxury Homes Series

High Style From the Finest Architects and Builders

Carolinas, Chicago, Florida

Specialty Titles

Publications about Architecture, Interior Design, Wine, and Hospitality

21st Century Homes, Distinguished Inns of North America, Into the Earth: A Wine Cave Renaissance, Luxurious Interiors, Napa Valley Iconic Wineries, Shades of Green Tennessee, Spectacular Hotels, Spectacular Restaurants of Texas, Visions of Design

Custom Titles

Publications by Renowned Experts and Celebrated Institutions

Cloth and Culture: Couture Creations of Ruth E. Funk, Colonial: The Tournament, Dolls Etcetera, Geoffrey Bradfield Ex Arte, Lake Highland Preparatory School: Celebrating 40 Years, Family Is All That Matters

Panache Books App

Inspiration at Your Fingertips

Download the Panache Books app in the iTunes Store to access select Panache Partners publications. Each book offers inspiration at your fingertips.

Panache Partners, LLC   1424 Gables Court   Plano, Texas 75075   469.246.6060   www.panache.com

INDEX